Touching Your Soul

A poetic journey through love and yearning

Ranadeep Bhattacharyya

India | USA | UK

Dedication

To the ones...
Who have woken up
With a parched heart,
Drenched in unsayable longing.
Who gaze at the stars
And wonder why life cannot whisper,
In moments of loneliness,
The address of one's soulmate?
Why must aeons pass
To meet the one
Destined only for you?

Acknowledgement

From the depths of my heart, I extend my profound gratitude to those who have been the bedrock of support and inspiration on this journey -

Judhajit, the catalyst whose unwavering belief transformed my scattered poems into the cohesive tapestry of this book—thank you for being the soul of my creative venture.

Sheetal, your faith in my art surpasses even my own; your encouragement has been a guiding light.

Madhusmita, for your endless words of encouragement that lifted me during moments of doubt.

Vaishakhi, our afternoons spent delving into verses will forever be cherished memories that shaped these pages.

Ricky Ji, for your precious time to provide me with your invaluable insights on the book and your suggestion for the title that perfectly encapsulates its essence.

To my dear parents *Rita & Rabin*, whose love and strength are the pillars upon which I build all my creative dreams, thank you.

My entire family— especially my sisters *Didibhai, Mi, Pu, Jonaki & Mithu*; my brother *Shubhadeep* and *Kabita Kakima*—your relentless cheerleading propels me to pursue my passions with zeal.

Lastly, to my lovers and memories that echo eternally. This book is not just my story, but a mosaic of all our shared moments.

Preface

Because...
They will never be yours,
They can never disappoint you.
They remain a perfect idol,
Forever worshipped from afar.
Whispering in lonesome solitude,
Bleeding hearts with bittersweet pain—
Unrequited love.

In the vast labyrinth of human emotions, few threads run as deep and persistent as longing, love, and the quiet ache of unspoken connections. This collection of poems, born from the depths of such emotions, is a tapestry of moments—some fleeting, some eternal—woven together with the fragile strands of memory, desire, and introspection.

Each poem in this anthology reflects the universal yet profoundly personal journey of the heart. It is a journey of waiting and wandering, of holding on and letting go, of discovering oneself in the shadow of another. These verses traverse the realms of time and space, blending the mundane with the cosmic, the transient with the eternal, and the tangible with the ethereal.

Unrequited love lingers through these pages—not merely as an absence, but as a force that shapes, moulds, and transforms. It speaks of a love that exists not in possession but in persistence, not in culmination but in continuation. A love that dwells in silences, in the spaces between words, and in the quiet resonance of memories long past.

This book invites you to pause and immerse yourself in these emotional landscapes. Allow the words to echo within you, to stir memories of your own loves and losses, and to remind you of the indomitable spirit of the heart that dares to hope, even in the face of uncertainty.

Whether you find comfort, resonance, or reflection in these pages, know that these poems were crafted with an openness that seeks to connect with the innermost recesses of your being. As you read, may you discover not only the poet's voice but also your own, whispering back through the lines.

Welcome to this journey of the heart.

INDEX

All We Left Unsaid

I long to see
The day
When forgotten promises,
Misjudged extinct volcanoes,
Flare back to life—
Embers rekindled,
Molten truths flowing once more,
Illuminating the shadows
Of all we left unsaid.

Prisoner Of Spring

Through every breath,
You enter my being.
I usher you deep—
Warmly, willingly—
Into the ruined citadels
Of my bleeding heart.
We watch each other
In the stillness of the night.
You traverse every cell of me—
An endless moonless sky,
Where stars send shivers down
The paths we once walked.
Red-washed walls of longing—

Are you a dream or a nightmare?
With each breath, I wager hope:
Perhaps this time I can hold you,
Safe in me, for eternity.
Forever, Prisoner of Spring,
Even blossoms now feel
Like wreaths.

A Trace Of A Memory

My treacherous thoughts,
Lonely blue nights
Sans the moon.
I closed my tired eyes,
Breathed into the pain—
A pain I mistook for your love.
Amidst the engulfing darkness,
I see a hand, stretching toward me;
Familiar, yet distant—
A trace of a memory
I cannot recall.
Breathing out the burden of the past,
I reached to touch the hand,
Only to find
I was holding myself.

Since then,
My words no longer
Speak your name.

Thorns & Roses

Red from the roses
Of our night-long passion
Bled into the silences
Of our night of separation.
The scent of your moist, warm body—
To me now, the bittersweet perfume of a rose.
Tell me,
Can a thorn
Ever escape its destiny
With the rose?

If You Had Dared

If you had dared,
The world might have cared.
We could have had a future—
A dream to nurture.
My silly heart,
Fragile, bare,
Would not have ruptured,
If only you'd dared.

Waiting For You

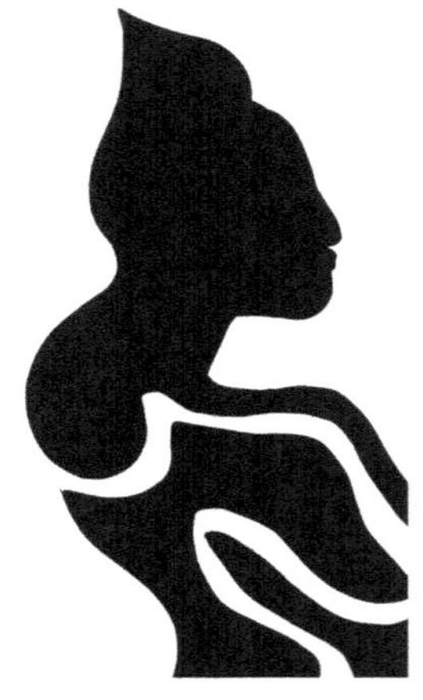

Spring will flourish you—
I pray it does.
But I no longer wish
To witness its bloom.
The fragrance of your flowers
Lingers in entangled memories,
A life of regrets,
A portrait of eternity.
A need I outgrew
Last winter,
While withering alone,
Waiting for you.

Patience

Perhaps
The nights are a bit longer now
But
I am used to waiting for long,
May be
Patience is a declaration of faith,
A vision
From the future holding hand
A reassurance
Of walking on the right path
Feeling
The golden hues of twilight
Even
Under the burden of darkness.

Blank Verse

You color me
In hues unknown,
Stories I had never
Called my own.

To rhyme together –
Not in our destiny.
I am the blank verse
In your poetry.

Rusted

So long I
Have wanted you.
I have rusted
In my own
Imagination of us.

Afterthought

It's not that
I didn't love you—
It's just that
I didn't love myself
Enough.

Illicit

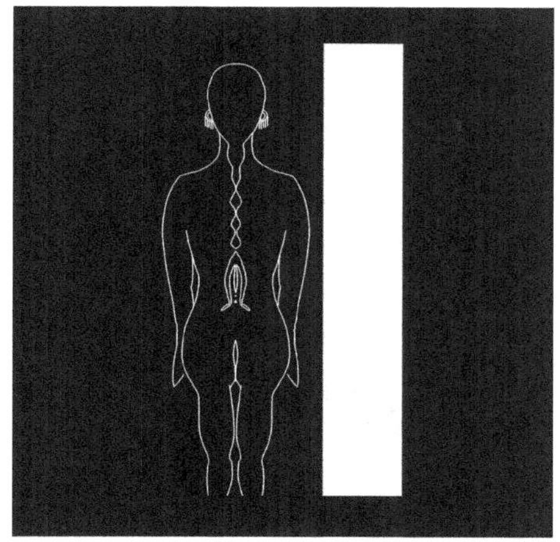

Illicit
They name our relationship!
Though I prefer the name
Freedom.

Phone Gallery

What you were
Is fading.
What you are
Is awakening.
You and I—eternally tied
By our souls,
Yet distanced
By life.

Now,
We remain together—
Only
In our pictures.

You & I

All that has been lived,
Breathed, and let go,
Still resonates somewhere.
You & I—
Our moments long rendezvous,
All are present, tender in spirit,
Long after we cease to exist.

In the same way light that shimmers,
Warm and alive,
To reach us beyond
The clutches of time and space,
From stars long dead—

We exist,
Eternal,
In our unreality.

Beyond the illusionary web
Of ever-flowing time,
Beyond fact, fiction, and reason,
Beyond the realm of vision and sound—
The eternal dance of self-discovery
Plays on,
An unending quest—
Will my soul
Ever find you?

Your Shimmering Blues

Eternal traveler,
Lonely soul,
Hungry for love,
Wrapped in time,
Beyond consciousness.
And yet,
All of my being
Melts into silhouette skies,
Beneath your crimson sun.
Transient waves of life—
Let me pause,
Take a deep breath,
Before I merge once more
Into your shimmering blues.

Just For Tonight

Our nights
Of lights.
In this crowd,
We forget all
That keeps us apart—
Snuggling into the pullover
Of anonymity,
Let's set aside
Our fears,
Morality,
Confusions,
Just for tonight.

Let us lose ourselves
In the crowd of ordinary,
Committing the follies
That passing time
Begs of us.
In anonymity,
Let our animals meet,
Untamed in their wilderness.
This lone night,
We step into our shadows—
Silhouettes amidst the crowd.

What Relationship Do We Share

Remember once, you asked,
"What relationship do we share?"
You pestered me with concern,
"What name shall we give it?"
My lengthy nights are spent
Searching for an answer.
I swim through the bondages
Of countless mortal names
That life's journey begets,
Struggling to find a constant

In this eternal sea of change.
Cruel time, gives and takes away all in jest,
Here, every name is put to test,
And futile feels this quest
To name what can only be felt.
Yet, since you are adamant still,
I have only this to say—
Call yourself the one
Who now resides within me,
As my sleepless, gut-wrenching pain.

My State Now

My state now?
I feel an intense burning in my body—
A pain that sears through my entire being,
As if I am water,
Placed to boil on the burner of my memories.
The truth is:
The fire is real,
And so is my peril in its grasp.
When I burn and boil, I am agitated—
My mind, always anxious.
Yet, amidst this turmoil,
What once troubled me from within
Slowly begins to evaporate from my core.

I cannot feel it now—
The scars of boiling water
Are too raw to bear.
But perhaps,
What leaves me in vapor and steam
Was never meant to stay.
I must learn to let it go.

When has the river lamented
The clouds that float above it?
The patient river, wise and aware,
Knows the eternal truth:
"What goes away today
Will return as rain tomorrow."

What belongs to you
Can never be truly taken away.
It may travel the farthest distances,
But its *karma* is to return to its source.
Until then,
The water keeps boiling,
The river keeps flowing,
Eternally bound to its destiny—
Its inevitability.

You

You—
Whom I can't see
Anywhere
Yet feel every moment,
Everywhere.
You, tormentor of my soul,
An unannounced breeze,
Sending shivers through
Unsuspecting, naive leaves,
Making them dance
Under your invisible spell.
You!

We Will Always Have Us

If tomorrow
We no longer know each other,
We will always have us—
Safe in the eternity of time.

A tree's memory of bloom
Is forever etched
In its rings.

The Darkness We Share

You take the stars;
I keep for myself
The healing light
Of the moon.
We parted with smiles.
Neither of us realized
We still had to share
The looming dark night—
A black hole to our souls,
An eternal sky
Of nothingness.

What You Still Mean To Me

Beyond reason,
Beyond doubt,
Beyond all the whys and hows,
You remain hidden
In this safe place within me.
Let others vie
For pleasures and glory,
For the divine light and bliss,
For perfect love
And picture-perfect lives,
Residing together for eternity
In the valleys of heaven.

I am content—
With just a moment of you,
Lighting me up
In all my darkness.

Our Only Picture Together

"Looking good together... Say cheese."
Little did your gleeful photographer friend
know—
The moment he proudly captured
Was the carcass of a love, ruptured.
I had embraced you—
A universe with its black holes,
Dancing in glittering meteor showers,
Unaware of stars blurring out,
Dying a slow death

Behind their own light.
You said you still cared,
Apologetically—
Like this moment, frozen in time:
A whole of you,
And just a fragment of me.

That Night

You could have been
Anyone that night—
An idealized version
Of my collective imagination.
But you were you,
And I was me—
And the red of your sangria
Still stains the color of my lips.

I Was There

The sweet scent of white jasmine,
Rustling leaves on a summer night—
Our panting bodies,
Entwined in zillion promises
Of a future we dared to claim.
You took it all away,
Along with you.
Only that kohl-smeared night remains,
Gradually engulfing me
In its broken promises.

I was there —
Always.
But where were you?

We Will Meet Again

Why fear death, separation, or the future,
When the crimson sun,
Her blushing sky, and hidden stars,
Waves that bear witness to distant shores,
Hold our story in their whispers—
A shining pearl
Cradled in the heart of an oyster.
On our next brief visit to this Earth,
Let us seek that pearl once more,
And together,
Give life its worth anew.

A Perfumed Night Of Intoxication

Remember—
Naked on silken sheets,
Breathless with passion,
In a perfumed night of intoxication,
You casually asked:
"Where do roses find their flaring red?"
That night,
The rouge of my lips
Paint your cheeks crimson.

Alas, your heart
Beats in my red veins,
And blood oozes
Long-forgotten embraces.
Perhaps it's the thorns of memory
That blush the rose red.

Water & Ice

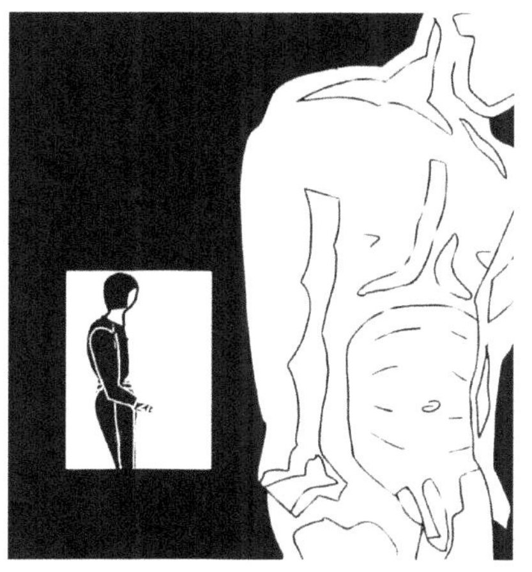

Neither the will
To leave was mine,
Nor the will
To stay was yours.
We feigned enough—
Melting into each other,
Water and ice,
Bound to transform,
Never to hold.

Candle's Devotion

If tomorrow, you and I
See different futures,
Remember the candle—
Burning through the night,
Toward her own end,
To keep our glass castle
Safe from darkness.

Unveiled

Perhaps it's time
To let go of the veil
I hide behind—
To let you see me,
Just once,
For who I am,
And not the shadow
Of what you imagine me to be.

Where To Find Me

If tomorrow,
You no longer find me
By your side,
Look for me
In your wilderness.

A Love That Exists In The In-Between

The skipped beat of my heart
Each time you DM me a picture—
Your yellow-blooming smile
From a land my soul calls home.
Somewhere,
The "we" I secretly imagine
Feels real.
Feels complete.

A Thief Without A Heart

What have you turned me into
With your love?
I can't even bring myself
To curse the road
That misled you
To a safer refuge
You now call home.
Drenched in eternal wait,
Yet burning like a vulnerable flame,
I sing through the night,
Cajoling the very road

To lead you back to me,
Just once.
Don't thieves have hearts at all?

Beyond Vermilion Boundaries

Deep within me,
Deeper than you've ever reached,
Lies a part —
Untouched, unearthed, unspoken.
Beyond vermilion boundaries,
A throbbing reality of desires
Burns quietly.
Only the sky is my witness—
Would you ever
Trickle down as rain?

Tides Of Longing

Silently, secretly, I have suffered—
A thousand fantasies,
Longing for you.
Like a wave,
I rise and break,
Unable to kiss
The steadfast promenade.
Slowly, I disintegrate,
Evaporate—
Invisible to you,
I dissipate from life itself.

When Worlds Collide

Silences find their voices,
The past beckons hope,
When chance plays god
And, our worlds collide—
Once more.
Stealing an ounce of love
From a bygone memory,
The warmth of your kiss
Still runs deep in my veins.
Even earthquakes feel gentle
When our worlds collide.

If Only You Could Stay

If only you could stay,
Nights would embrace days.
The scent of your absence
Blooms in my barren existence.
Dewdrops tremble in dreams,
Daffodils of passion sway.
Oh, if only—
For the sake of magic—
You could stay...

Across Aeons, For You

I have come too far—
Across seven seas,
Through countless aeons,
Forsaking pleasures and securities,
Everything I once called my own,
Everything that defined me.
Forgetting the way back,
I have come too far—
Just because you called,
Just because you wished to see me.

The Stream Within

Deep inside me,
You flow like a careless stream.
At times, I dive into you;
At others,
I sit by your bank,
Lost in deeper contemplation.
Which glacier feeds you within me?
Will this stream
Ever meet the sea?

A Gift Never Received

I am yet to receive
What was addressed to me.
Has it lost its way?
Or been delivered
To someone more fortunate?
Perhaps it was never meant
To reach me.

Yet, why do I feel
That no one deserved
To belong to it
More than me?

Lovesick

It wasn't even an affair.
The raindrops dried up
Before they could kiss the ground.
Yet, the nights tease your thoughts,
And my being
Reeks of you.

The Art Of Misunderstanding

The things you said,
You might not have meant.
The things you heard,
I might not have screamed.
Our relationship is such
Only mutual misunderstanding
Can make it work.

The Summer Of Us

True,
The summer of our love
Is long lost.
Aeons have washed away
Hopes from our dreams.
Yet today,
When we met,
My heart betrayed me—
A caged bird,
Flapping anxiously,
Once again longing
For its sky.

Sublimation

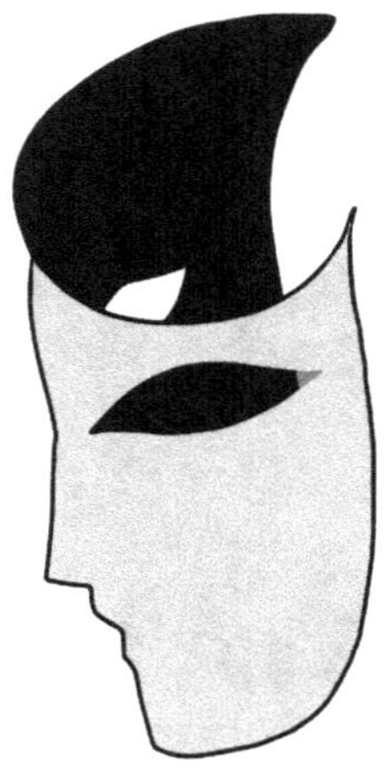

What we once had
Between us
Has found rebirth
In my verses today.
Like camphor and dry ice,
We sublimated—
Straight from solid to vapor.
Do you ever wonder
If we had not jumped the queue?
Perhaps, as liquid,
We could have flowed forever.

The Folly Of Sight

Eyes are—
Windows,
Memoirs,
Light,
Soul,
Doorways,
And streams.
Yet, unwise—
Foolish enough
To fall in love
At first sight.

Crumpled Echoes

Crumpled,
There lies that white page—
The one where you
Scribbled my likeness.
Musings on a moonlit night,
Reddened by my heart's blood,
Lost in the crevices of time.
Me,
On that blank page,
Still lies there—
Crumpled.

An Unfinished Story

Petals of alstroemeria,
Untouched,
Wither away in silence,
Tucked between the pages
Of last year's diary.
Our week-long hopeful dreams,
Secret rendezvous behind closed doors,
The essences of us—
Faith and promises,
Starry melodies,
All slowly fade
Into oblivion.
We remain...
An unfinished story.

The ink of our words,
Once bold,
Now smudged by time,
Carries whispers of conversations
We never completed.
The walls that bore witness
To our stolen moments
Stand untouched—
Silent,
Yet heavy
With the echoes of us.
The fragrance of alstroemeria
Still lingers faintly,
A ghost of what once bloomed.
And though the pages turn,
Though the seasons change,
Somewhere, in the quiet of night,
The unfinished lines
Of our story
Long to be written.

Evergreen

As the years pass by,
You grow evergreen—
My constant in the fleeting seasons,
Unfazed by time's relentless flow.
Your essence,
Once tender as a budding leaf,
Now stands strong—
Rooted in memories,
Flourishing in the light
Of all we once shared.
Storms may come,
Winters may linger,
But you remain,
Evergreen.
A presence unyielding.

The Paradox Of Desire

My not wanting you—
Anytime, anywhere, anymore—
Makes me want you—
Even more.

Isn't it possible
To begin again—
Like each year's
Summer, winter, and rain?

Love Beyond Understanding

As you, my love,
Strive and toil—
Forever seeking to understand us,
Diving into the depths of analysis:
Right and wrong,
Alternatives,
Tallying the balance sheets
Of our transient seasons
Of hate and love—

You only lose me
In the labyrinth of your mind.
Meanings, feelings, flow—
All so important to you—
Fade away,
Like twilight dissolving
Into oblivion.
Ours, us, we—
A painting,
Meant to be expressed,
Never to be understood.

Out Of Sync

Pages of existence,
Scribbled with thoughts—
A memory, a fantasy,
Coloured in hope.
An incomplete picture,
Fading gently toward a destiny
Etched aeons ago.
If only the characters knew—
When to close a chapter,
And when to open
Another book.

Note To Self

All I knew
Of who I am
Fades into mists—
Treacherous illusions,
Shifting truths.
Hands of time—
Are you moving, or am I?
Crowded graves,
Abandoned hearts,
All searching for answers.
Stay or leave?

Stay, if words
Still hold your hand.
Leave—but where?
Melting masks,
Charring souls—
The only way to love
Is to embrace its ephemerality.
Here now,
Gone in a blink.
Naive life,
L'esprit de l'escalier.[1]

---

[1] L'esprit de l'escalier is a French phrase that translates to "staircase wit." It refers to the phenomenon of thinking of the perfect comeback or clever remark too late, often when descending the stairs after leaving a conversation. It reflects the bittersweet realization of missed opportunities and unspoken words.

Tides Of Time

What you were
Is fading.
What you are
Is awakening.
You and I—
Eternally tied by our souls,
Yet distanced
By the currents of life.

Eclipse —
How long
Will you last?

The Address Of Mirage

My address?
Ask the sand grains
Breathing within the pages
Of the book I was reading
While we drove away
Into our wilderness.
Do mirages in the desert
Have their own address?

Healing

Since the woman within me
Felt the weight of disappointment,
Bore the scars of betrayal,
And endured wounds inflicted
By the men who surrounded her;
I had no choice but to rise—
To become the ideal man for her.

The Road To You

Travelers,
Lost in an eternal quest,
Entangled in webs of delusion—
Spiral cycles
Of births and rebirths.
When will this thirst be quenched?
How far must I walk
The path
That leads to you?

The Allure

Black dreams,
Burning desires,
Hardened truths,
Haywire expectations,
Forbidden passions—
Am I in love,
Or simply addicted
To my nightmares?
Perhaps both.

Embers Of Change

Something is changing
Within—
Don't you feel it?
Embrace it with kindness,
Accept it with grace.
For in the end,
Joy will be found
In the gentleness of a breeze,
The warmth of fading sunlight,
And a heart
That never regretted loving.

Cruising Online

Endless sky,
A lonely star.
Dense forest of desires,
A hungry tiger on the prowl—
Chasing shadows,
Searching for a flicker of light.
Like the wind, I seek you,
Wandering through
The glow of endless screens.

In long digital nights,
From profile to profile,
I search—
Looking for a home
In fleeting houses of glass.

Unshackled

Today,
Choose yourself.
Today,
Break free from every shackle.
Today,
Let your past
Finally become the past.
Shed every burden,
Every weight
That holds you back.
Today,
Step into your true destiny.
May all that is unrequited,
All that is not you,
Fall away.

The Warning I Ignored

Yes, I am guilty.
I didn't heed your warning—
"Don't fall in love with me,"
You had so casually beamed.
I now recall
That fleeting instant—
The arrow pierced deep within.
I became yours to keep,
Without demand,
Without barter,
Without commitment.

Your smile evoked
My heart's quiet submission.
From that moment,
There was no turning back.
Lifetimes, aeons,
Reincarnations—
I keep walking,
Scorching sand beneath my feet,
Through endless desert storms,
Searching for your likeness
In every soul I meet.
Longing for the one—
The beaming face,
The voice that once warned me
Not to love him.
Hardened heart, failing age,
Ravages from healing time—
The now me has a truth to share:
My love,
That could never be yours,
Still roams in unnamed graveyards,
Waiting for its fulfillment.
It meets you,
Time and again,
Growing beyond what universes can contain.

What if my love
Is a gift you never claimed?
What if my love
Arouses in you feelings
You can't bring yourself to face?
Is my love unacceptable
Because it does not have a name?
I love you too much
To let it burden you with shame.

The Light Within

Why is it
That what nature conceals
In darkness
Emerges in shades of white?
The pearl inside the oyster,
Bone within the body,
A grain of rice,
A bud of cotton,
A *totala* flower—
Is it not the same with love?
What the heart buries,
Unseen and unspoken,
Grows pure,
Flourishing in shadows.

Who meditates
On the womb of longing
Transforms darkness
Into light?

Ruins Of A Love

It starts the same way every night.
She wakes in a cold sweat,
The sound of splintering wood
And crashing bricks
Echoing in her ears.
The ache of loss sits heavy on her breast,
But beneath it, something deeper churns—
It was a figment of her imagination,
A fragile projection of hope,
A sanctuary built with borrowed dreams.
The house haunts her—
A reality she believed in,
A love she thought was indestructible.

And yet, every night,
She stands beneath the collapsing walls,
Each thud of brick, a cruel reminder
Of futures abandoned mid-construction.
For now, the dreams persist.

But perhaps—
If a house can crumble,
Can it not also be rebuilt?
Somewhere, amidst the debris of yesterdays,
Lies the foundation of tomorrows.
And though the silence she craves
May not come easy,
One day, she will wake to find herself
Not beneath collapsing walls,
But beneath a boundless sky,
Ready again to build her home.

The Ache Of Fading Moments

Isn't it one of life's greatest ironies—
We only truly value the present
Once it slips into the past.
Why do we find ourselves
Longing for what we can no longer have,
While failing to cherish
The fleeting beauty of moments
As we live them?

Perhaps it is the nature of time—
A relentless teacher,
Whispering wisdom too late,
Leaving us to marvel at
What was,
And mourn the richness
We didn't know we held.

Edits Of The Heart

Some love stories don't fade—
They're made of jump cuts,
Abrupt transitions,
Moments spliced together,
Leaving us breathless
In their imperfect rhythm.

Companions On The Road

Cars are lonely beings,
Destined to wander,
Moving through life,
Thirsty for oil, leaving trails of gas behind—
A monotonous existence, devoid of affection.
Forbidden to touch,
To brush against one another,
Their solitude is etched
In the unyielding rules of the road.
It seems love is their curse.
When cars passionately collide,
It spells their doom—
A love so intense, it consumes them entirely.
Or perhaps it is a love of a different kind:

A silent, enduring companionship,
Side by side on unknown, undulating roads.
They travel together, yet never too close,
Careful not to harm one another.
Is this restraint their tragedy, or their grace?
To love by staying apart,
To accompany without collision—
Perhaps mine is the love of wanderers.
The love of cars.

The Weight Of Imagined Lives

We suffer,
Not solely from the weight of reality,
But from the lives we craft
In the boundless dimensions of our minds—
Worlds always brighter,
Paths always more thrilling
Than the one beneath our feet.
It is in these imagined realms,
Where possibilities stretch infinitely,
That dissatisfaction is born.
The present pales in comparison
To the dazzling fiction
We endlessly replay within.

Perhaps it is our curse,
This unyielding creativity,
To dream of better lives
While stumbling through the one we live.

The Eternal Ache

At birth,
The ones who welcome you—
Smiling, joyful, embracing your first cries.
At death,
The ones who bid you farewell—
Somber, reflective, holding your last breaths.
In most cases,
These two sets of people
Are strangers to one another.
The hands that cradle you at the beginning
Are not the hands that close your eyes
At the end.

And in between these two moments,
Life unfolds.
Connections are forged and fractured,
Love is found and lost.
And in the space
Between those who greet you
And those who see you off—
Life happens,
And the ache is born.

Freedom To Love

I love you
Because there is nothing you can give me.
No gifts, no promises,
No weight of expectation.
I don't seek anything from you—
Not comfort, nor answers,
Not even the assurance of your love in return.
And in that absence,
There is freedom.
A love that exists
Not to fulfill a need,
But simply to be.

Saudade

So many poems I have written,
Futile offerings
To lovers who will never know of them.
Each line, a whisper,
Each stanza, a yearning—
Words spilled onto the page,
Never meant to reach their ears.
They linger in silence,
Tucked away in the folds of notebooks,
Scattered across crumpled scraps of paper,
Or buried deep
In the quiet corners of my phone.

Perhaps it's better this way.
To love in secret,
To let the verses live on their own,
Unbound by the weight of expectation
Or the burden of being understood.
For isn't that the purest form of love?
A quiet devotion,
A poetry written for the sake of feeling,
Not for the sake of being heard.

Cartography Of The Heart

The heart is a map.
Cities built and cities demolished,
Citadels guarding old insecurities,
Ruins of regrets ever mounting.
Yet, somewhere, a sapling of hope sprouts—
A quiet promise that tomorrow,
You will find your way through it,
Winding roads leading you back
To the place we call home.

The Ones Who Remain

Some people are meant to stay,
To walk alongside you,
While others arrive only
As bittersweet lessons—
Leaving behind footprints of growth
And the ache of their absence.

The heart is the only place
Where one can truly grasp this.

For there is nothing more shattering
Than the breaking of trust,
The echo of promises turned to dust

And yet, within that same heart,
Lies the extraordinary.
The broken pieces find their way back,
Guided by those rare souls—
The ones who help you gather love once again.
They are not just companions;
They are guardian angels in disguise,
Assembling the shards with quiet grace,
Teaching you how to bloom
Where life once seemed barren.

The Endless Becoming

The end
Is the beginning—
A circle unbroken,
Where all we leave behind
Becomes the seed
Of what lies ahead.
The final note,
A prelude in disguise.
The last step,
The first of a new journey.
The end
Is never truly the end—
Only the beginning

Of becoming.
What if we are all just orgasms—
Ephemeral bursts of existence,
Moments of rapture,
Constantly dissolving,
Reforming,
Seeking completion
In the infinite cycle of becoming.

The End

www.ingramcontent.com/pod-product-compliance
Lightning Source LLC
La Vergne TN
LVHW011029200726
843509LV00011B/1230